YO-BRB-652

God's plans for me are good and filled with hope for my future.

"For I know the plans I have for you," says the Lord. "They are plans for good and not for disaster, to give you a future and a hope."
Jeremiah 29:11

God, I thank you that you are executing your plans in my life. I know they are good and filled with things beyond my wildest dreams. I submit my plan to your plan.

PROMISES OF VICTORY

God
supplies all
of my needs.

And this same God who takes care of me
will supply all your needs from his glorious riches,
which have been given to us in Christ Jesus.
Phillipians 4:19

Lord, you know my needs and my deisres.
I trust you and know you will take care of them.
I give you my worry & fear in exchange
for your peace.

**Nothing I do, and
nothing anyone does to me,
will ever separate me from
God's love.**

No, despite all these things, overwhelming victory
is ours through Christ, who loved us. And I am
convinced that nothing can ever separate us from
God's love. Neither death nor life, neither angels
nor demons, neither our fears for today nor our
worries about tomorrow—not even the powers of
hell can separate us from God's love. No power in
the sky above or in the earth below—indeed,
nothing in all creation will ever be able to
separate us from the love of God that is revealed
in Christ Jesus our Lord.

Romans 8:37-39

PRAYER

Thank you God that nothing can separate me from
your Love. Let me experience Your love today,
and let me show it to others.

PROMISES OF VICTORY

God gives me
a peace the world
cannot take away.

I am leaving you with a gift—peace of mind and
heart. And the peace I give is a gift the world
cannot give. So don't be troubled or afraid.
John 14:27

God I come to you knowing that your peace
is something no one can steal. God please guide me
and give me that peace today.

I am
free from
sin and death.

For the law of the Spirit of life [which is] in Christ
Jesus [the law of our new being] has set you free
from the law of sin and of death

Romans 8:2

Continue to reveal to me Lord, the freedom that you
have given me. Let me live according to your grace
and not feel the condemnation of the law.

I am far from oppression and fear does not come near me.

"You will be firmly established in righteousness:
You will be far from [even the thought of]
oppression, for you will not fear,
And from terror, for it will not come near you.
Isaiah 54:14

God I come to you knowing that your peace
is something no one can steal. God please guide me
and give me that peace today.

PROMISES OF VICTORY

I have the
mind of Christ.

"Who has known the mind of the Lord so as to instruct him?" But we have the mind of Christ.
Ephesians 1:4

Lord I thank you that my mind is clear and open. You have given me the ability to learn and understand. You give me clarity on decisions and wisdom in the direction I need to take.

PROMISES OF VICTORY

I have the peace of God that passes all understanding.

SCRIPTURE

...and the peace of God, which surpasses all understanding, will guard your hearts and minds through Christ Jesus.
Phillipians 4:7

PRAYER

Lord I thank you that you have given me peace. No matter what happens around me your peace surpasses my circumstances.

PROMISES OF VICTORY

The greater one lives in me; greater is He Who is in me than he who is in the world.

You are of God, little children, and have overcome them, because He who is in you is greater than he who is in the world.

1 John 4:4

Jesus come and live inside me. Give me faith and understanding to know that you live in me and there is no obstacle that I can not face because you are with me.

PROMISES OF VICTORY

I have received the spirit of wisdom and revelation in the knowledge of Jesus, the eyes of my understanding being enlightened.

I keep asking that the God of our Lord Jesus Christ, the glorious Father, may give you the Spirit of wisdom and revelation, so that you may know him better. I pray that the eyes of your heart may be enlightened in order that you may know the hope to which he has called you, the riches of his glorious inheritance in his holy people,

Ephesians 1:17-18

Lord I thank you that you are guiding my path. You have given me wisdom to discern what is the right path for my life as I seek you.

I have given, and it is
given to me in good measure,
pressed down, shaken together,
and running over.

. Give, and it will be given to you. They will pour
into your lap a good measure—pressed down,
shaken together, and running over [with no space
left for more]. For with the standard of
measurement you use [when you do good to
others], it will be measured to you in return."
Luke 6:38

God give me the spirit of generosity,
and bless the things that I have given
to come back to me in great abundance.

I can do all things through Christ.

I can do all things through Christ
who strengthens me.
Philippians 4:13

Thank you Jesus for living inside of me.
Give me power and confidence knowing
that I can do all things through you.

I am God's masterpiece, created to make a positive impact in the dark world.

For we are His workmanship, created in Christ Jesus for good works, which God prepared beforehand that we should walk in them.
Ephesians 2:10

Thank you Lord for guiding my steps
and giving me the confidence to know that
you are proud of me and I am on your mind.

**Because of Jesus,
all I do is win!**

Yet in all these things we are more than
conquerors through Him who loved us.
Romans 8:37

Lord, I acknowledge that all things
come from you and you cause everything
that I do to be a success.

I am healed because of what Jesus went through on His way to the cross.

But He was wounded for our transgressions,
He was crushed for our wickedness [our sin, our
injustice, our wrongdoing]; The punishment
[required] for our well-being fell on Him,
And by His stripes (wounds) we are healed.

Isaiah 53:5

Lord, you care about everything in my life,
including my health. Please heal my body
and remove all disease from me.

**I will not fear.
God has given me a
spirit of power, love,
and a sound mind.**

For God has not given us a spirit of fear, but of
power and of love and of a sound mind.
2 Timothy 1:7

God make me brave today. Give me peace
in my mind. Give me peace in my heart.
Let me love you more and love others more.

PROMISES OF VICTORY

I am a servant of God.
No false accusation, allegation
or claim against me is valid.

No weapon forged against you will prevail, and
you will refute every tongue that accuses you.
This is the heritage of the servants of the Lord...
Isaiah 54:17

Lord you alone are my defender.
No evil thing that anyone says,
does or claims against me will stick.

I have favor
that surrounds me.

SCRIPTURE

For surely, O Lord, you bless the righteous;
you surround them with your favor
as with a shield.
Psalm 5:12

PRAYER

God increase the favor in my life
Let me have supernatural favor
with those I run into today.

PROMISES OF VICTORY

Because I am a believer in
Jesus, I can go to Him for
strength and peace.

SCRIPTURE

The name of the Lord is a strong tower;
the righteous run into it and are safe
Proverbs 18:10

PRAYER

God I come to you for supernatural strength and
peace. Give my mind rest and give me confidence
knowing you are orchestrating all things.

I will have peace at night and sleep like a baby.

When you lie down, you will not be afraid;
when you lie down, your sleep will be sweet.
Proverbs 3:24

God I come to you for supernatural strength and
peace. Give my mind rest and give me confidence
knowing you are orchestrating all things.

I am loved by God.
He is thinking about me today,
and will give me peace of mind.

Let the beloved of the Lord rest secure in him,
for he shields him all day long, and the one
the Lord loves rests between his shoulders.
Deuteronomy 33:12

God show me that you are with me today.
Bless the places that I go and give me peace of mind.

**Because I love God
and desire to know Him,
He answers my prayers.**

If you abide in Me, and My words
abide in you, ask whatever you wish,
and it will be done for you.
John 15:7

Thank you for hearing my prayers,
and answering them according
to your plan for my life.

PROMISES OF VICTORY

Because I live according to the word of God, He will never leave me. He will always provide for me and take care of my children.

I was young and now I am old, yet I have never seen the righteous forsaken or their children begging bread. They are always generous and lend freely; their children will be blessed.

Psalm 37:25

God thank you for taking care of me.
I know you will not forget about your child.
Continue to reveal your love to me.

I seek the Lord,
and He provides for me.
I have everything I need!

Fear the Lord, you his saints, for those who fear him
lack nothing. The lions may grow weak and hungry,
but those who seek the Lord lack no good thing.
Psalm 34:9-10

God, I honor you and your word.
Please provide for me in ways that only you can.

God give me everything I need to be a success today and everyday!

And God is able to make all grace abound to you, so that in all things at all times, having all that you need, you will abound in every good work.

2 Corinthians 9:8

God, I submit to you and recognize that all success comes from you. I give you the glory for everything you have given me!

PROMISES OF VICTORY

God's blessings towards me are overwhelming. My dreams aren't out of reach or too much for God.

Now to Him who is able to do far more abundantly beyond all that we ask or think, according to the power that works within us, to Him be the glory in the church and in Christ Jesus to all generations forever and ever. Amen.
Ephesians 3:20-21

God reveal to me what you want for my life. Give me the faith to believe for it and the perseverance to pursue your plan.

PROMISES OF VICTORY

When I come to God in prayer
and expect Him to answer,
He always will!

All things you ask in prayer,
believing, you will receive.
Matthew 21:22

God thank you for hearing my heart and answering
my prayers. Continue to give me the faith to ask for
your will to be done in my life.

God has given me the power to work, make wealth, and be a success in every area of my life.

But you shall remember the Lord your God, for it is He who is giving you power to make wealth, that He may confirm His covenant which He swore to your fathers, as it is this day.
Deuteronomy 8:18

God give me the strength to do more for you and the power to create wealth to sow into your kingdom.

PROMISES OF VICTORY

If God has called
me to do it, He will
make sure it happens.

Faithful is He who calls you,
and He also will bring it to pass.
1 Thessalonians 5:24

God I have trusted in your plan.
I will continue to trust you
as you bring it about.

I am brave. I am strong.
I can face what is ahead of me,
because God is with me!

Be strong and courageous, do not be afraid
or tremble at them, for the Lord your God
is the one who goes with you. He will not
fail you or forsake you.

Deuteronomy 31:6

Give me courage Lord.
I know you are with me.
I know you will not fail me.
I trust in you.

PROMISES OF VICTORY

**Because God loves me,
He will take care of all my
troubles, worries, fears,
failures, and stress.**

Casting all your anxiety on Him,
because He cares for you.
1 Peter 5:7

God I give you all my troubles,
worries, fears, failures and stress.
Take it. Remove it. Replace it with peace,
love, hope, and joy.

God values me more than any other thing He has created. If He has guaranteed to take care of them, He has guaranteed to take care of me.

Look at the birds of the air, that they do not sow, nor reap nor gather into barns, and yet your heavenly Father feeds them. Are you not worth much more than they?

Matthew 6:26

God I know you care for me.
I trust you will take care of me.

God makes me strong and healthy, both physically and emotionally.

For I will restore you to health and I will heal you of your wounds, declares the Lord.
Jeremiah 30:17

God, I have faith that you can and will heal me.

When I am weak, God is strong. He gives me what I need to keep going!

And he said unto me, My grace is sufficient for
thee: for my strength is made perfect in weakness.
Most gladly therefore will I rather glory in
my infirmities, that the power of Christ
may rest upon me.
2 Corinthians 12:9

God give me strength when I'm weak.
Lift me up when I'm down. Heal me
when I'm sick and give me joy when I'm sad.

God fills me with joy and strength today!

Do not be grieved,
for the joy of the Lord
is your strength.
Nehemiah 8:10

Lord, give me a supernatural
joy today. Give me a positive attitude
and grateful heart!

God gives me His wisdom, His understanding, and His perseverence to make it through the day.

Counsel is mine and sound wisdom;
I am understanding,
strength is mine.
Proverbs 8:14

God, give me wisdom
and understanding today.

When I come to God, He will give me a second wind. I will have unhindered strength and perseverence.

Yet those who wait for the LORD will gain new strength; they will mount up with wings like eagles, they will run and not get tired, they will walk and not become weary.
Isaiah 40:31

God I come to you for a renewed strength. Give me determination and power to continue to execute the plans you have for me.

PROMISES OF VICTORY

I can overcome any and all temptation.

No temptation has overtaken you but such as is common to man; and God is faithful, who will not allow you to be tempted beyond what you are able, but with the temptation will provide the way of escape also, so that you will be able to endure it.
1 Corinthians 10:12-13

Give me strength to overcome temptation today. Increase the desire to know you more Lord, so that sin looks ugly to me.

When I am going through tough times, I am not defeated. God is purifying my faith.

Consider it all joy, my brethren, when you encounter various trials, knowing that the testing of your faith produces endurance. Blessed is a man who perseveres under trial; for once he has been approved, he will receive the crown of life which the Lord has promised to those who love Him.

James 1:2-3, 12

I look to you God when
I'm going through hard times.
Do a work inside of me.
Purify my faith.

God has made my life brand new. I'm not the same person. People who knew me will see a difference, and people who meet me will meet the One who lives inside me!

I waited patiently for the Lord; and He inclined to me and heard my cry. He brought me up out of the pit of destruction, out of the miry clay, and He set my feet upon a rock making my footsteps firm. He put a new song in my mouth, a song of praise to our God; many will see and fear and will trust in the Lord.

Psalm 40:1-3

I'm so in love with you God. Thank you for saving me! Thank you for making me new!
I honor you with my life.

When I ask for forgiveness,
God forgives me and there
is no more guilt or shame.

SCRIPTURE

If we confess our sins, He is faithful and righteous
to forgive us our sins and to cleanse us
from all unrighteousness.
1 John 1:9

PRAYER

Forgive me, Lord, where I've missed it.
Give me your desires and
let me hear your voice.

PROMISES OF VICTORY

I trust God, and He is the author of my life story.

SCRIPTURE

Trust in the Lord with all your heart and do not lean on your own understanding. In all your ways acknowledge him, and he will direct your paths.
Proverbs 3:5-6

PRAYER

I trust in you Lord.
I want you to write my story
and make my plans. Give me the faith
to follow and know you more each day.

I'm seeking God, and He directs and gives me the desires of my heart.

Delight yourself also in the Lord;
and he will give you the
desires of your heart.
Psalm 34:4

I seek your counsel first, Lord.
Transplant my heart for yours.
Grant me the desire you have for my life.

When I let God draw the blue prints of my life and trust him to build it, He will build a marvelous building.

Commit your way to the Lord,
trust also in Him, and He will do it.
Psalm 37:5

God, take control.
Be my guide.
I want you to run
my life, not me.

I have peace God will handle every situation I face. In my patient waiting, He is working.

Rest in the Lord, and wait patiently for him:
do not worry because of him who prospers in his
way... but those that wait upon the Lord,
they shall inherit the earth.
Proverbs 37:7,9

As I wait for you to prove
yourself faithful, Give me peace
that you will take care of me.

When God has given me a promise to stand on, it will come to pass, in His timing.

SCRIPTURE

For the vision is yet for the appointed time;
it hastens toward the goal and it will not fail.
Though it tarries, wait for it; for it will certainly
come, it will not delay.
Habakkuk 2:3

PRAYER

God give me the perseverance and faith
to see your promises come to pass.
I love you Lord and know you alone can bless me.

PROMISES OF VICTORY

**As I patiently pursue
the things of God,
He is good to me.**

The Lord is good to those who wait for Him,
to the person who seeks Him. It is good that he
waits silently for the salvation of the Lord.
Lamentations 3:25-26

God you are good.
Your mercies are everlasting.
I submit my life to your will.

**God's timing is perfect.
As I wait on Him, I can rejoice
knowing that He hasn't
forgotten me.**

As for me, I will watch expectantly for the Lord;
I will wait for the God of my salvation.
My God will hear me.
Micah 7:7

I wait on you Lord. You are all knowing and all
powerful. I know you have not forgotten me.
Remind me today of your love and faithfulness.

My children have been raised
with Godly principles and
a knowledge of salvation.
They will not forget
or run away from it.

Train up a child in the way
he should go, even when he is old
he will not depart from it.
Proverbs 22:6

I pray for my children - keep them safe and healthy.
Give them a desire to know you Lord. Pursue them.
Let them find you and find salvation.

When my children
are taught of God,
their path is successful.

All your sons will be taught of the Lord;
and the well-being of your
sons will be great.
Isaiah 54:13

Lord, as I teach my children the ways of your kingdom,
let them understand that all success comes from you.
Bless them and give them a knowledge of you.

The knowledge and love
for the things of God will
continue in my family for
generations.

The lovingkindness of the Lord is from everlasting
to everlasting on those who fear Him,
and His righteousness to children's children.
Psalm 103:17

God continue to bless my children
with the knowledge of you and your word.
Do not let them depart from you.

God will never quit on me. He will continue to mold me into what He wants me to be.

SCRIPTURE

Being confident of this, that he who began a good
work in you will carry it on to completion
until the day of Christ Jesus.
Philippians 1:6

PRAYER

Lord, thank you for not quitting on me.
Mold me into what you want me to be.
I want to be a masterpiece dedicated to you.

God has forgiven my sin and forgotten my past.

When you were dead in your sins and in the
uncircumcision of your sinful nature, God made
you alive with Christ. He forgave us all our sins,

Colossians 2:13

Thank you for your forgiveness God.
Take away my guilt and shame and let me
see myself as you see me - forgiven and loved.

I don't have to fear death.
I know that I am saved and
will live forever with Jesus.

"I give unto them eternal life" I give them
eternal life, and they shall never perish;
no one can snatch them out of my hand.
John 10:28-29

God take away my fears.
Show me that you care.
Demonstrate your love for me today.

I believe in Jesus and have no cause to feel shame, guilt, worry, or fear from things in my past.

Therefore, there is now no condemnation for those who are in Christ Jesus,
Romans 8:1

God remove from my heart the shame, guilt, worry, or fear from things in my past. I give my life to you. Renew me.

God will not fail me.

He will not leave me.

I do not have anything to fear.

The Lord himself goes before you and will be with
you; he will never leave you nor forsake you. Do
not be afraid; do not be discouraged.

Deuteronomy 31:8

Go before me today God.
I trust in you. I fear not.
I have peace in You.

PROMISES OF VICTORY

God's forgiveness knows no limits. His consistency is immeasurable.

Your mercies are new
every morning: great
is your faithfulness.
Lamentations 3:23

Thank you Lord for your forgiveness today.
I repent of the things I've done against you.
Be with me today and help me by your
Holy Spirit to live a life pleasing to you.

What God says
He will do for me,
He will do!

Faithful is he that calls you,
who also will do it.
1 Thessalonians 5:24

God I trust you are doing a work in me.
Continue to guide me. Continue to bring
about your plans for my life. I want you to
have your way in my life.

Today the God of Hope fills me with joy and peace through believing.

SCRIPTURE

May the God of hope fill you with all joy
and peace in believing, that you may abound
with hope by the power of the Holy Spirit.
Romans 15:13

PRAYER

God I believe that what you have said,
you will bring to pass. Thank you for filling
me with joy and peace today as I trust you
with my future.

PROMISES OF VICTORY

**Every promise that God
has made will come to pass.
I will hold on to His promises
and believe to see His
goodness in my life.**

"It is the same with My word. I send it out, and it
always produces fruit. It will accomplish all I
want it to, and it will prosper everywhere I send it."
Isaiah 55:11

God I believe that You are true to Your Word
and faithful to Your promises. Today I hold on to all
that You have said and stay in joy knowing that
You will bring it to pass.

PROMISES OF VICTORY